# Let's Track the Storm

## What Will Happen?

I0812964

Dale Dixon

COMPUTER SCIENCE For the REAL World™

Rosen Classroom™

There are clouds.

The sky is gray.

Is a storm coming?

I turn on the TV.

The weatherman shows a storm.

He uses a weather map.

The storm is coming!

# Words to Know

clouds

storm

TV

weather map

weatherman